HOLDING TIGHT TO GRAVITY'S TAIL

HOLDING TIGHT TO GRAVITY'S TAIL

Lorraine Merrin

RaineMtnArts
Castle Rock, Washington

HOLDING TIGHT TO GRAVITY'S TAIL

RaineMtnArts
Lorraine Merrin
PO Box 397
Castle Rock Washington 98611-0397

Illustration: Debbie Lou Harrison/Silver Lake, Washington
Sawnceea Rae Thomson/Portland, Oregon

Layout/Formatting: Wally Merrin

Printing/Binding: Gorham Printing
3718 Mahoney Drive
Centralia Washington 98531

Merrin, Lorraine
Holding Tight To Gravity's Tail / Lorraine Merrin
1st Edition
ISBN 978-0-9829696-0-1

ACKNOWLEDGMENTS

Early versions of some poems in *Holding Tight To Gravity's Tail* debuted in literary journals. My thanks to the following journals, and a bear hug for Joseph Green, who retired from Lower Columbia College, Longview, Washington, at end of term, 2010. Joe was, among other things, Faculty Advisor for students working on *The Salal Review* which is published at end of term each school year.

U.S. 1 Worksheets Volume 55, 2010 *Slow Hand*
Moon Journal Volume 13 Issue 2, Summer 2008
This Is For That Arizona Girl
Rattle #22 Volume 10, Issue 2, Winter 2004
Around The Corner Of Midnight
Rattle #25 Volume 12, Issue 1, Summer 2006
The Annual Officers' Club Party Suddenly Comes To Life
The Salal Review Spring 2008 *The Devil Pounds The Door*
Spring 2006 *He Tends Roses Now*
Spring 2005 *A Blood Orange Sky*
Spring 2004 *Girls' Night Out*
The Great American Poetry Show, Volume 2 September 2010
Around The Corner Of Midnight

* * *

Love and applause for Wally Merrin, computer guru. (Couldn't do it without him!) Love and hugs for my mother and dad and many thanks for their patience.

Love and gratitude to Stellasue Lee, friend, editor, and mentor; to Ruth Holzer who is sharp of eye and ear; to Wendy Kosloski and Shirley Bailey for encouraging my creative efforts.

Love and hugs to Mary Kaye Nelson, Mary Gale Lush, Marguerite Smith, Mary Lee Troseth, and Chris Seward, my fan club. A big grin and "thumbs up" for Mary Helen Ber, who one day just appeared in the wide middle of my life. Bear hugs for B. D. (Skip) Giannini, who is no longer lost, but found.

CONTENTS

SECTION 1: IN THE ROOM WHERE I DREAM OF WAR

SECTION 1 CONTINUED

SECTION 2: HOLDING TIGHT TO GRAVITY'S TAIL

SECTION 2 CONTINUED

HOLDING TIGHT TO GRAVITY'S TAIL

My friend, Kathy, admitted to me once that she had had a perfect childhood. She had been loved and fed, protected from life's worst storms. She was, in fact, a secure, happy child.

In spite of this setback, Kathy turned out okay.

—lm

IN THE ROOM WHERE I DREAM OF WAR

Dust

Prayers,
hymns for the dead,
the fortunes of men—
hang on the slightest breeze.

Mere dust underfoot
carries the bones of your
father's father's father,

holds the wisdom of civilizations
across the universe, knows answers
to questions not yet conceived.

This finely ground courier recalls
every secret, carries proof
of each crime—
        it is the essence of *all*.

This dust has traveled halfway
around the world; holy grit polished
in the sea or thrown to the wind,

carried in shoes, pockets, on the fleas of dogs.
It has nourished potatoes, coffee beans, squash.

This dust is your midwife, your memory,
your salvation, your shroud.

Into The Wind

Sometimes
you just have to put your head down,
grit your teeth, walk into the wind

no matter what's happening
around you, inside you.

Sometimes
you have to let your eyes glaze over,
see nothing, because you cannot bear it.

Sometimes
you must let the blood run—
        let it run from your mouth
        after biting your tongue.

When reason fails
and the veins of love are bone dry,
rise up then, with a great rush of wings.

Burn the feet of the enemy,
rip out their tongues,
set them free to study peace.

Blade's Edge

In a hiss of steam
and the shimmering fierceness
of forge and fire,

the blade is freed,
released from the heat
raw and angry.

Spirits collide, meld,
as he strikes and shapes
the stubborn steel heart

to perfect angle and heft;
a truce between beauty
and function.

Burnished flames draw back,
steel cools; the Bladesmith
once again

finds balance
between her edge
and his soul.

Foxhole

In a forest of shadows
he crouches in snow
aching for sun.

Hungry, he dreams of meat
in a sleepless dark and hugs
the myth of love close,

gathering warmth from the breath
of a lover he's never held
under a sun he cannot see.

In a forest of shadows he clutches
at faith remembered from a childhood
as lost to him now as love and sun.

Exile

Three nights in a row
he's dreamed himself
in a prison camp.

He keeps his eyes lowered,
never looking in the guards' faces,
aiming for balance between
deference and disdain.

He holds his ground,
keeps his own counsel,
calls up faith, then calls again.

Why or where or who
makes no difference.
He cares only that he is caged

and refuses to sleep,
else he sleep a prisoner
and answer to *slave*
when he wakes.

Ashes

With dawn
they counted more dead,
tightened thin fingers
around survival.

At night
they wrapped themselves
in an ice-blue moon for warmth,
filled empty bellies

with memories of hot soup,
slept with one eye open, that
Death would not carry them off.

After,
the names of the dead
swirled around them in acrid ash
every Sabbath sundown.

Their children grew up
in the company of ghosts
without lullabies or nursery rhymes.

They grew like honeysuckle and ivy,
taking root in dreams of sunlight
and clean air—

they are testament to the history,
keepers of the faith; the names of the dead
lie familiar on their tongues and comfort them.

Spiders' Silk

He's away again,
the warrior she loves—
        she hugs his pillow,
        wears his favorite t-shirt
which is way too big for her
but it smells like him,
        and she can imagine
        his arms around her.
She plays the answering machine
just to hear his voice,
        refuses to wash his pillowcase
        for fear of washing him away—
of somehow breaking that fine thread,
like spiders' silk— that binds them,
holds them tight in any storm.

Of Dust And Dreams

In the black and white photo
of my mother, she wears
her best dress with a locket framed
in the vee of the neck, and her

thick chestnut hair curls around
her pretty face. It is 1943,
the year my mother graduates
from high school.

Her shy smile hides the loss
of a stolen childhood, denies
the shadows of The Great Depression.
She believes in a better future,

she believes in herself,
and she's not telling what her dreams are:
those dreams are all she has to get her through
and damned if she'll tell and lose them.

Souvenir

Of my father, I have only
a pair of opera glasses
inlaid with mother-of-pearl,
taken from a home in Germany
during World War II.

I imagine they were
left behind when a
terrified young man packed
a clean shirt and trousers,

hoping
against all reason
he would not be sent away
on the last ride of his life.

The opera glasses belonged
to *Mama* or perhaps, *Oma*,
and my father would have found them
as American troops entered Berlin.

Without thinking, he dropped them
into a pocket as tanks rolled,
victors marched and waved,
throwing chewing gum

and chocolates
to children and pretty girls.
I wonder if he thought of
the pretty girl back home,

if he missed her at all.
Of my father, I know this:
without thinking, he dropped
odd bits into his pockets

and kept marching.
Without thinking,
he rearranged our lives
as if we were naught

but odd bits; he, the victor,
we, the spoils of war,
picked up here or tossed there
for his own amusement.

Carry On

At dawn his mouth opens:
winged screams fly out, flailing
at the root of pain; tiny teeth bite at speech.

Ghosts fill the folds of his days,
sit with him, share his beer, offer
their own superstitions.

She serves love and prayers
with meals of meatloaf and mashed potatoes;
she throws all her fight against his war, swearing
to rebuild their lives around his broken body.

His demons confront her
in the hallway, behind doors, inside cupboards—
they spit, hiss, curse, and chatter among themselves.

She knows they wait for her
to stumble over them in the dark,
come upon them in her jewelry box,
find them, sprawled, on her laundry room floor.

She's hanging on.
She'll have him back again.
She will have him back.

In Dreams The Prisoner Of War Makes His Way Home

To find home,
mark the sun, then

follow the contours of land,
the sweep of valley, the run
of river.

Seize the moon, hold it ransom
before a field of stars to find
that soft flatness of belly, familiar
arms, the scent of ginger or clove.

Never give up, never look back;
whatever it takes, move forward.
Whatever it takes, get home.

Hug the curve of spine
as two cradle together,
petal and leaf,

the perfect arc of bodies
so much like the curved gate of heaven.

Chasm

Sometimes
she doesn't know him at all
though he sits in the same room.

It is, she says, as if he went away
and never returned.

Sometimes she misses him
though he sleeps
at her side.

It is, she says, as if she's alone
only more alone than that.

At night her dreams twist
'round the moon;
she never dances now,

rarely speaks aloud—
there are few words left
and they'll only fall, frail

and unheard,
into the deep chasm
that has claimed her life.

The least he could do, she says,
is give back her heart.

Devil In The Pawn Shop

I once knew a sax player
        who could make that horn *wail.*
Like Gabriel, he'd blow,
        but tender, smooth enough
to break your heart,
        make you grateful for every
kind word you'd ever heard,
        every bowl of soup
you'd ever eaten.
        One night I asked him
how long those tunes
        been singing out their pain.
He said he'd been at it
        ever since he'd gotten that horn
from a serpent, in trade for an apple.

Sexy Beast

He's got a slow, southern smile,
dimpled chin, amber-honey eyes.
Without a doubt,
this farmer's son can hold his own,
skilled at reading sky, land,
stranger, and knowing well
how to track and trap:
she never had a chance.
She's a beauty,
dancing and flirting in a smoky
Baja *cantina* full of artists, drifters
and *gringo* sailors looking for a good time.
Dancing and joy are free
and so is she,
before his ring and her promise,
before dawn, as they fly
down the coastal highway
chasing a laughing moon
in a '54 Chevy convertible—
that sexy turquoise beast she loves
almost as much as she loves him.

Addiction

Memories crawl through his veins,
jump and twitch under his skin:
every firefight, every hard-won hill,
eyes beseech— or stare, empty as the sky.

Time moves on and fortunes change,
but not for him— never for him. He
wanders the streets and alleys in town,
holds his hill,

because God knows
he's got his orders—
and God knows
there's not a needle big enough,
or a bottle deep enough
to kill that wretch inside,
those damn eyes just staring.

Summer Of Love

Thick as thieves, they were that summer,
traveling up and down the West Coast
in ones and twos, in droves, piling off

old school buses at rest stops
and truck stops, with backpacks
and sleeping rolls:

restless *flower children* in long hair
and threadbare tie-dye, hitching rides
to the mystical City of Light.

High on smoke and fog they sought
adventure and a future; a psychedelic,
copacetic new world— *Love, not war.*

The *Children of Aquarius* wanted to see
the world, wanted the world to see them.

Sun-Blind

Lightning could strike him down,
he'd never let on it was coming,
just like his Papi's switch whistling
        through the air—

that boy'd set his jaw, grit
his teeth, and never flinch.
No way in hell he'd cry.

The old man would be so riled
he'd damn near spit nails; in the end,
nothing to be done but walk away.

The sky was still full of stars
the morning that boy stole off,
leaving little, taking less.

He disappeared into the west—
making them wait, sun-blind,
as they watched for his return.

One Hundred Degrees

outside and the Navy
cut him loose, sent him home
to a wife he no longer knew,

two boys who needed a daddy
and a country convinced he was
a baby-killer.

One hundred degrees outside
and the flames of hell burn bright
in the steel mill.

While he works,
he imagines sitting on a sea wall
holding a cold beer, watching

bikini'd perfection stroll by.
He didn't love her, that little
California gal, though he can

still feel her lips, smell her hair.
At least, he should have said goodbye.

The Sailor's Ma'am

He cannot ask me
to say goodbye
to watch him walk away
watch the ship sail out of sight

He can't ask this of me
because like kelp
we're tangled into one breath
a single heartbeat

I send my love with him
I send talismans
sea charts
prayers

He swears to love me only
promises gifts
spices and jewelry
opulent fabrics

He is sea and tides,
I am sand—
in his absence,
unsettled
shifting
fearful
of slipping away
as if I never was

Fidelity

He once called her name in a voice
full of tenderness and awe, not quite
believing such a beautiful creature
belonged to him, loved him.

He took her to his bed—
captain of a ship on a deep, wide sea
and made her wife, made her mother,
left her always waiting.

Her ashes now settled with the dust
on the mantle, he is lost, captain
of a ship without compass or rigging,

waiting for the sea to reclaim her own,
pull him to a cold breast, currents
holding him between wife and mistress,
a faithful husband at last.

Home To The Sea

War bit and chewed,
ripped skin and pitted bone,
gulped him down, then
spat him out, defiled.

Approaching the sea
he calls up the wind, communes
with waves, sends shrieking gulls off
carrying cryptic messages.

Moments later, saltwater washes away
the last fragments of his guilt.

The sea croons,
beckons with wide, foamy arms.
She will be mistress of his mortality.
He knows she cannot save him—
        perhaps, if she's kind,
        she'll forgive him.

Wind Across The Rez

1968

Snow dusts branches
and muddy ruts in the road.
The silence is broken by a rush
of wings, a coyote's yelp.

He is gone now, lost
in the white man's war,
where shades of green and fragrant blossoms
struggle to mask napalm-scarred hillsides,
ghosted villages, plundered crops.

A warrior's son, he took the fight
to the enemy, bravely counting coup,
willing to die for those who hissed *Chief*
or *Injun* and couldn't forgive him
for not getting stone-drunk with them.

He used a rifle, a machete and his wits.
Back home, the family used food stamps,
federal commodities—weevils in the flour, mold
on the cheese. The old truck held,
with baling wire, bits of Ace bandage and spit.

Here in this quiet place, the ponies run
through the canyon and his breath
brushes your cheek like wind.

After

He keeps a low profile,
black linen shirt, black beret,
and travels incognito,

wanting only to be accepted
now that he's finally home
from the great jungle war,

where for a while he was lost
and had to gather himself
together again—

frayed bits of faith, blinded eyes,
a leg here, a scrap of trust there,
the torso ripped and bleeding,

all painfully collected and reassembled
into a mosaic of beating heart and long,
raggedy-moon nights.

The One Who Will Not Be Broken

At canyon's rim,
the wind blows through me.
The sun rides low, throws

fading copper light
on the ponies running
through the canyon—

they've run this trail
for as long as grandfathers
can remember.

In the shadows,
a brother gone to war, riding
his own pony, lasso spinning out

to circle the neck of the prettiest,
the fastest, the one, like him,
who will not be broken.

Into The Bruise Of Midnight

Tonight
he'll want as if famished
and set before a feast

Tonight
will be like no other night
the darkness will be different
we will be different
        the same but changed
        the way hours change

from morning into noon
from noon into dark
        and he'll need
        the way a guilty man
        craves innocence

This warrior bound so tightly to war
to foreign terrain and spilled blood
        now must walk
        into the bruise of midnight
        loose his grip
        hold love in a gentle palm

In The Blue Smoke

of the night's cigarettes
in the lingering heat of warm beer
and bodies too close
he'd ask her to sing for him
just one song
before he called it a night

One song
to take him home
before the war made pretty girls
and children dangerous
before every back alley
became a hot zone
before the flashbacks
lit up the room erasing sleep

With just the two of them
and walls full of secrets
he'd play something slow
something that old piano
could bite into   then they'd dance
to the beat of their own hearts
until the sun came up

Semper Fi

He's in Marine green,
tall, handsome, too good
for the government to waste,

too young to have a choice.
He reaches for her, his hands
grasping for the security

of home and family.
One last hug, a quick prayer,
Vaya con Dios, hermano, and he

leaves for war, half a world away.
All the way there and back,
there will be only thin air

to hold him,
turned to tiny droplets of sweat
when he reaches for courage.

---

(1) Go with God, brother

Trash Day

Skate wheels   metal grinding concrete
the sound of incoming rockets
dogs yelping and growling

Trash truck rumbling
gears grinding   brakes squealing
the swamper shouting to the driver

as giant jaws open
and teeth mash and chew
as trash falls   is torn and crushed

bits and pieces of lives
flung out into the street
and he cannot sleep

this weary soldier
he cannot sleep in this soft bed
with clean sheets and sounds of battle

crashing through an open summer window
though he left the constellations of war
and their carnage half a world away

Milk Cartons

We'll kick ass, he said,
I'll be home before you know it.
I heard he kicked ass, alright,
but he didn't come home to me.

I nearly found him once,
so close, but he'd skipped out,
just missing my inquiries, another
phone disconnected, letter undelivered.

Sometimes I think I should put
his picture on milk cartons.
People could study his face
while eating cereal, a sandwich:
Little sister searches for big brother.
Have you seen this soldier?

Love And War

for Bernard Dominic Giannini / Vietnam

Hey, big Marine! Me love you pretty,
me love you good!
Hey, big Marine! Me keep good hooch
for you. Me love you good!

In paradise, so much beauty
        explodes in the smell
of rich soil and singed flesh,
        such hot contrast to the cool greens
of lush, jungle exotica.

Watch all around you, beware
        the delicate, blooming bodies
of suicidal young beauties
        with their woeful eyes
and wet, hungry mouths.

They'll suck your heart out,
        leave you to die.
One kiss, and you both fly into the air,
        slowly drifting back to earth,
weightless, like bright bits of feathers.

Your hours are filled with danger
        'til Death comes,
perfect white teeth gnashing, ripping,
        tearing the muscle and heart of you,
your life whispered away on the slightest breeze.

I Drew Maps

If I could, I'd have saved him
from war and loneliness and dreams
that still haunt his nights.

I'd have given him anything—
I drew him into my lungs to keep him
close to me; like vapor, he vanished.

I gave him the run of my heart
thinking love would keep him safe.
I drew maps for him,

offered poems for the dead
and prayers to heaven; like a cloud
of opium, he vanished.

I couldn't know he'd fall into hell,
leaving me to tend the gates,
feed the coals.

Storms Rising

I know where he comes from,
what he left behind, why he fears darkness.

I let him breathe me in
breathe, I say, *just breathe.*

I know how difficult the struggle,
how bitter the taste on his tongue.

I let him taste me,
sweet as almonds and honey.

I know his secrets; shards of memories
blind him in bright light, cut his feet in the dark.

I recite incantations to quell the storms
rising from his tangled dreams.

I loved him once
I will love him again and again—

until he can travel on his own into any country,
across any sea, oblivious to storms rising.

In The Room Where I Dream Of War

the walls are tumbled down,
bereft of windows.
The rusty smell of blood hangs
on the air and sorrow springs
from tattered remnants of old letters.

There are no words for this,
the searching
not knowing
my prayers spilled across cracked
pavement, under bridges and into gutters,
with the litter of the hopeless.

After all these years he is now
not lost but found, yet time
has formed a canyon beneath our feet,
the trails unmarked, overgrown.

If I look away for just a moment
he'll become mist over the river,
a leaf falling to damp earth.

He Took Me From Sleep

to say: 3:00 a.m. and the fireplace is cold.
I'm sorry to steal you away from warm sleep
and, likely, better dreams than I've had lately.

There's no hope of putting yesterday back together,
I know, but I saved all the pieces just in case—
got 'em right here in my pocket. If we work together
we might find tomorrow before the weekend comes.

I ain't high, but lord, I need to hear your voice.
I wish I could touch your face, see the lamp's light
shining your hair like it does.

A Soldier Once Stood

He doesn't use his legs now,
        he scoots around
on his bum, lifting himself with arms
        tight as barbed wire.
He's got new legs and they work
        pretty well, but he says it's hard
to think about them in the morning
        when he first gets up because
he wants to pee
        and doesn't want the fitting
and buckling and mostly,
        the remembering.
Sometimes, you can catch him
        wheeling around town
in his motorized chair,
        the one his brother helped him
modify with tuck 'n roll upholstery,
        black leather, red trim,
and as much chrome as they
        could fit—
a '64 Bug's battery and tail lights give
        his wheels more visibility after dark.
He says he sure misses quiet,
        when it's finally cool after
the heat of day
        and even birds are still,
but that pure silence hangs
        just out of reach;
he can't get free
        of rockets and bullets,
the scream and chew.

The Annual Officers' Club Party Suddenly Comes To Life

Late Summer 1973

Women in cocktail dresses
feign interested politeness
as their men wheel and deal.
        She glides into the room
        like honeysuckle vine,
        conquering in full bloom:
black leather knee-high boots,
a mini-skirt, stretch-lace body shirt,
and hair down to here.
        Every man's head swivels
        and feminine radar
        sounds an alarm.
Her flirting is like
skin or green eyes
or breathing.
        The guys fall hard
        and she's not even
        beautiful.
The pulse of the room quickens
as a whisper of turmoil
stirs the air—
        feathers
        have been ruffled,
        and all she's done is walk in.

She Didn't Mean To Send Him Away

so far
that he couldn't get back.

His last night home, and she
never meant to send him off
wrapped in incomplete sentences,
promises swaddled in questions.

In truth, she loved him too much;
wanted him so, she could barely
breathe when he was in the room,

and half afraid he'd been conjured
from the heat and draught
of summer's lightning nights.

Damn the war,
damn the distance between them
and all the words they couldn't say,

as if their own language
was suddenly foreign, their tongues
split and hissing doubts and invectives;

and the enemy—
damn the enemy
for stealing their youth,

for stealing their lives,
for *being*.

Collateral Damage

He returned to her
after a long, dry absence,
brittle, thin as glass.

In summer's heat his pain
is an ache, a dull fever, bone deep.
Winter sharpens the pain so it wears
on the soul, cuts right through.

Sometimes his eyes give it away
or the set of his jaw:
        Their lives twisted into the rubble
        of youthful dreams; love blindsided
as rockets explode behind his eyes
and screaming wounded share their bed.

He was young and strong when the jungle
snatched him, cracked his spine.
Now they endure, caught up in a war
over thirty years gone.

Sayonara Saigon

He'd been in Tokyo long enough to know a girl who loved him, another who lived with him, and one who had his child. He knew the first girl loved him, wondered about the one who lived with him— maybe all she wanted was a steady paycheck and a guy who didn't hit her. The one with his child didn't love him, never had, but she was a good mother despite snide remarks about her beautiful but round-eyed baby.

New orders: Sayonara Tokyo and the doe-eyed girl who loved him cried. The one who lived with him kept the apartment and a pretty, pouty girl moved in with her. The one who had his child asked for help paying bills, kissed him when he promised. From Tokyo he was shipped to Saigon where the beer was hot and the women dangerous. He tended the young and brave, watched helplessly as the light dimmed in their eyes— freedom's lifeblood spilled onto wet, muddy ground, or wafted away on a warm breeze.

No young girls loved him in this place. No one lived with him or had his child. His youth fell away, hit the dirt under a badly lit operating table. His faith curled into a tightly wound ball, fell, rolled into a wide, red-stained river. His heart ached; the pain made it hard to breathe.

When he said Sayonara Saigon he didn't say it loudly or wave goodbye to pretty girls. He didn't feel anything at first, went into shock, crimson spread across his chest. He tried to laugh but choked instead. Then, good soldier to the end, he stepped into the cradling closeness of his final resting place, lowered the lid, slept.

No Bone To Pick

He had no bone to pick with anyone. No angry words, no imagined slights, no need to prove a damn thing. He knew who he was, where he came from, where he belonged.

He set the house on fire with laughter, with love, with projects and silly games, until he went to war, having no bone to pick with anyone, but following orders, doing what a good son does, what a good soldier must.

While he was away his fire burned low, sputtered and nearly died, so many tears fell upon it. The house tried to help: the walls stood erect, surrounding those he loved. The floors cracked and buckled, but held fast. Roots of fear, of frustration and anger grew up and spread, sought to break through, snatch away the ones he left behind. Even the dog snarled and chewed to stay free.

The day he returned, his house sat on its corner lot under a wide open sky as blue as his eyes, surrounded by sunlight and daffodils newly emerged near each side of the front porch. On the third day after his return, dawn threw a softly-colored palette across the sky. Dew drops sparkled when first light found the corners of window panes. The house smoldered, wisps of gray floated up from the floors until orange-tinged heat waves shot through the roof. Window glass cracked, doors hung askew, their hinges broken and the wood charred. The blood on his hands dripped, stained. His eyes were full of pictures that escaped their frames, stole his sleep. His throat was full of stories he couldn't translate.

His Heart Wanders In Wilderness

Loss has burned his lips, blackened his tongue.
His eyes mirror a wild country; his heart holds
the half-naked women, their hungry children.

This paradise turned killing ground
is forever scorched, starved. Roads
are paved with want, rivers quench no thirst

and the rice baskets are filled with weevils.
He was a warrior, sired by a warrior clan,
gone into battle without doubt or sorrow.

He gave the best of himself—
for the sake of those tearful women
and their thin children, leaving me alone

yearning for his arms, his lips, the promises
we made. Even now, thirty years down
the road from that war of his,

he returns to live under my rib cage
counting each breath I take, chastising me
for being angry, or for wanting what I cannot have.

A Yard Full Of Roses

11 September 2001

In late summer's
early-morning coolness
windows shatter,
black smoke billows;

screams, sirens,
brick and glass
explode,
soar, spin,
crash to earth.

He is flying, floating, falling.

He thinks wife, child,
a yard full of roses,
a new red tricycle
he must bring home tonight.

Flying, floating, falling.

Where?
Where's the shiny tricycle?
Ribbon streamers
on the handlebars
and a bell.

Ordinary Things

If she lights a candle, two candles,
how many *Hail Marys* will it take
to bring him home,
        to bring him home alive,
        God, but it's hard
        alive and in one piece
        all this waiting.
She imagines awful things,
then is terrified they might happen.

The house is quiet now, settled into the night's chill,
resigned to standing guard under a blind moon.
The kitchen clock softly ticks off this night's
sleep allotment as she finishes wrapping and packing

small items: pictures drawn by the kids, photos
of the gang at the beach, chewing gum, toothbrushes
and paste, a paperback mystery, paper and envelopes,
new pens, favorite snacks, new socks, a deck of cards.

She fills packages with love to protect him,
sends everyday things to an ordinary guy
knowing that wherever he is, there will be
nothing ordinary about his day.

        At mail call his name rings out
        and he reaches for her love.
        This is a good day to be alive.

Shake The Hand Of A Veteran
Hell, Buy Him A Meal

Winter wind cuts to the bone,
and the streets are tough.
There's no beauty in alleys

littered with garbage
and the flattened cardboard
of fragile lives.

There's no mercy
in the stony silence of frozen men,
once sons and soldiers, husbands,

now warmed by rot-gut booze
and thin dogs. In war it comes down
to blood and earth;

bruised hands hold tight to dust,
broken teeth sink into damp, black soil
savoring the thin margin between life and death.

In The Last Year Of Our Indulgence

we bought buffalo steaks,
mushrooms and cheese. There were art supplies,
three new books, Christmas lights.
In the last year of our indulgence, we didn't fret.

It rained that year, snowed a little. Spring
arrived in all her glory and life was good.
This year electricity has gone up,
firewood is more costly, bread and milk,
eggs, no sweets, and meat just once a week.

Property taxes rise and we worry about losing
our home and where would we go,
old people like us? The young couple down
the road: two young ones, a single paycheck,
hanging on to the American dream
but their grip is slipping.

Another year of tax cuts for the corporate elite,
tax shelters for the wealthy
and a war we cannot end, cannot win, didn't want.
Soon, even dreams of indulgence
may be too rich for our ruined veins.

How It Came To Be
That Democracy Fell To Its Knees

From smoke and ruin he came on the day after,
to lead us to a new country.

He taught survival in a land
ripe with wonder and chance,

holy in its unwritten history,
human in its possibilities.

We gave our freedom and our future
to a stranger's promises:

divine guidance, dumb luck,
a world still turning.

Not that it matters—
we were still breathing.

Divinity is thin, luck is thinner,
breath thinnest of all.

Breath but vapor,
life's fragile root.

Justice

A young wife stands alone,
a child at once says goodbye
and embraces myth.

Taps echoes off green hills
or *Amazing Grace* spills through
open windows.

If there is any justice at all
there must be a place—
    where the chow is good
    the girls are pretty
    a three-day pass is easy
    the rifles, the rockets, the screams,
    are far away.

In A Silence Thick With Questions

What's it like, I want to ask him,
how does it feel to be blown apart;
to find yourself one with wind or rain?

How does it feel
to be weightless,
without substance—

before the pain, razor sharp,
before the dead start calling your name?
What's it like to touch the stars, find
the path to heaven?

As you floated back to earth,
I want to ask him, did you
want to leave Moon's sky,

was your heart still here with me, or
was your bloody fist wrapped around a star?

Atlas, Weary

What great history have we lost
that we cannot recite the names
from our past

and what shall we do

now that we are old
and deaf
and nearly blind

with aching bones
and bad teeth
What shall we do

now that Atlas
has set down his burden
and wandered away?

HOLDING TIGHT TO GRAVITY'S TAIL

Highway

Every morning
there's a bus leaves from that corner,
heading for parts unknown.

It'll run down across the flat,
around curves and over mountains.
It'll cross bridges you thought burned,

slide into tunnels you thought endless,
and carry you right to the door
of that place you remember.

Every night
there's a bus leaves from that corner,
heading from here to there and back,

stopping and starting
at places you never
heard of—

or thought you'd never hear of again;
all those places you meant to get back to,
all those places you meant to forget.

The wheels burn up the highway
and the tires thrum, singing about life,
about death, and the ride in between.

Vagabond's Child

Sometimes
it can't be helped
it's in the blood
runs through the veins
like liquor
street drugs
or wanting rough sex
with a stranger

The heart is
restless
rootless
unable to stay
more than a few hours
a day
maybe a night
unable
to pledge allegiance
to place
or person
always
seeking the illusive
or the righteous
or love
or even
just something like it

The Lie

is seen, first in the eyes,
then in the hands fidgeting with keys
and pocket change.

It is memorized
before a nervous tongue licks dry lips,
before hollow words slide over teeth:

I can't take you with me now Tadpole,
but I'll come get you in a week or two.

He thought he could retreat,
step away as if he'd never been there,
never looked into those wide eyes.

It never occurred to him
that four-year-olds
have no word for forgiveness.

New Kid

She was a scrawny kid,
looked like an underfed puppy,
huge eyes taking everything in

and that grin, missing teeth,
when she realized the kids
really did want to play—

not put her out in left field
or make her close her eyes
so they could drop a frog

down her shirt
or run off into the woods
leaving her alone at dusk.

Holding Tight To Gravity's Tail

we hang on to the tilted edge
of what we know of home—
and all things safe,

for we find little safety
in a wider world filled
with all manner of grief
men serve up to other men.

Surely this isn't the country
in which I was born.
Even the sky is different—
clouds that once held dreams
now drift away, leaving holes for the stars
to fall through.

Good Girls

We speak in a language all our own
and only to each other; we've learned
when to be quiet, how to become invisible.

We know the fine grit of truth is lost
on a deaf wind, and darkness lives
in unexpected places—

it won't surprise us again.
We know the color of danger, its shape,
the sound it makes; we won't forget this.

We can carry our whole lives in the space
of a matchbox, every lesson hard won.

We are sisters; inside our womb of silence
we reassure each other—
        yes, we say, *we are good girls,*
        yes, we say, *we remain*
        virginal, still.

Home Suite

Home was full of boys,
brothers and cousins
who treated her roughly,
loved her in their way.

Home was full of gun-metal anger,
swollen emotions. The rules
could change without warning,
but the dangers were known.

She grew skilled
at deciphering foreign languages,
became adept in guerilla warfare,
evading mines strewn randomly
across the family room or on

the far side of the kitchen,
and detonated her own small
rebellions with military precision.
Home was where leaving was
expected and could not come

soon enough. On her own,
she is free, but slightly unstrung,
lacking the nourishment of *familiar*.

There's Always The Shouting

    and this month's lover will tell her
how sorry he is for any number of sins,
    and lie about stealing her tip money.

It won't matter how long this one stays
    or when the next one comes—

Her daughter knows the score.
Too young to be grown, too old
to believe in anything more honest

than a slap or a curse, she no longer
tries to remember their names
or proper sequence, these lovers

she no longer calls Uncle, who
change with the seasons of her
mother's moods.

Her daughter knows the score,
and she watches that door,
ready for trouble to walk in,

waiting for the chance
    to slip out, run like hell.

Obsession

His words
tangle in her ear,
his breath is warm

on her neck.
I'd slide right into you
if I could.

I'd curl around your heart,
hug your ribs,
let your blood

wash over me.
I'd let you carry me inside you,
and never need again.

Her breath catches,
her lungs suddenly tight.
Her heart

pounds
just before
panic sets in.

The Sign Says *Vacancy*

and she pulls in,
exhausted, too hungry to go on,
too full of nerves to eat.

Rain slams scarred asphalt,
wind rattles windows in their frames,
and neon lights blink and hum.

Restless, she listens to voices
and laughter through the walls, feels the heat
and tenderness of lovers in the next room.

Spreading a map under the lamplight,
she studies all those open roads,
as the plumbing grumbles that she

should return home where she belongs,
to sigh against him, settle into sleep,
know her place.

Like Smoke Rising

he reappears without warning,
refuses to fade into the past he belongs to.

A constant threat, he creates fear
with every breath, every step.

She's made an uneasy peace
with the war he's thrust upon her,

and treads carefully across a battlefield
littered with friends they once knew,

plans they'd made
and the bodies of stillborn children.

To run serves no purpose.

This place will be her home,
warmed with lamplight and laughter,

but she'll be watching
for smoke rising across still water.

At The Clinic

there's no difference,
it doesn't matter why or how
or even how far along—

if your life has turned
inside out, this will be
the last peaceful day you'll know.

Every day after this
will hold the child unborn,
your prayers for forgiveness,

and a sorrow like a hollow bell,
its deafening clang unrelenting.
This child without a name

will be named a thousand times,
held and fed and loved;
will always dance behind your eyes.

Even Painted Lips Mouth Prayers

Leaning against the wall in the shade,
hip cocked, showing a bit of leg
(blue-veined but still shapely)

she stands outside the discount store
over on Morgan Street, the noon sun
harsh on powdered skin and poison-red lips,

but her old bones ache in the wind,
so daylight's the time to be out,
slim as it is.

She smiles and flirts, seeking
a moment's notice, transient warmth,
in the swirl of laborers and sailors,

wives shopping with their innocent daughters,
and packs of schoolboys snickering
as they saunter past.

Her autumn has come so soon,
without warning, without pension.
Under rouge and mascara, layers

of silk and lace, she feels worn thin:
her prayers rise, only to fall back again,
clattering against the dreams of her youth.

Summer Love

He played small clubs and coffee houses
for drinks and tips and scattered applause.
I found it novel, my own singer
and thought him quite beautiful.

All that summer we flirted with love
and he sang for me, songs written
on napkins at 3:00 a.m., ballads
for lovers and lonely soldiers,

the words tumbling over and under a melody
bled from his own Gypsy-Croatian heart.
When the leaves turned, he asked me
to travel with him.

He was so dear, my summer love,
but he couldn't stay and I had promises to keep.
One more day perhaps? Another week?
No.   Life is *now*.

Players

That trendy new place
in town is where
the *in* crowd hangs
the place to be and be seen
ubercool

The new place
isn't necessarily the place for us
Nah, you and me, we're
much better off
back in the old neighborhood
where we know all the streets
and back alleys

we know what's real
we like the way we look
we know the players
and twenty-seven ways
to make it home in a hurry

Girls' Night Out

You gotta' walk on in there and look like
you own the place— and the place
down the block too.

You gotta' walk on in there and not give
a damn about trend-setters and go-getters,
'cause you got your own style.

Order your drink, sit and sip it slow
like you got all the time in the world,
'cause the world turns on your dime.

Order another drink, chat with the girls.
Never let on how you're about to die
locked inside that lonely quiet

just before dawn.
Walk on in there all razzle-dazzle
and never, ever let the bastards know

you'd trade your heart
for a promise so thin
you could see clean through it.

Around The Corner Of Midnight

He's gonna' drink that ale
and watch the action,
see what there is to see,
catch a dance or two if somethin'

long-legged 'n lovely catches his eye.
He's gonna' dance real close,
slink tight to her swivel 'n
just about die wanting to look

to see do I notice.
Then he'll sit with his boys,
his fingers pushing circles of wet
glass-sweat across the tiny table top

while he scans the room,
so he won't appear to be
in a hurry to strut over here.
Yeah, I see him over there,

hangin' out 'n lookin' cool
in tight jeans 'n gold chains,
but if he wants me, he's gonna'
have to show me just what it is he's got.

I ain't walkin' around the corner
of midnight for just any guy.
I only got one heart 'n right now
it still belongs to me.

Good Girls And Outlaws

One day you're walkin' down the street
mindin' your own business
and the next thing you know there's trouble
right there in front of you and no way
to walk around it or get behind it

cuz you know you're interested—
you were hooked when you saw him
two blocks away and ain't nobody
gonna' believe you didn't want

to meet him
you wanted to ride that Harley
you wanted your arms around him—
and now here he is
standin' right next to you
on the sidewalk outside the Foster Freeze
not even thinking whether he wants
chocolate or strawberry cuz he's lookin'
at soft caramel and cream right there
in front of him

He's The One

This one:
twenty-four and fearless
that body in those jeans
got to be illegal
draped across his Harley
like that

his hair's a little too long
but his grin'll blind Mother Superior
and those slim hips and long legs
on a dance floor—
why a girl can't stand up
proper her knees gone all weak
watching those moves

and sometimes
after the day's work
after dinner and the dishes
he relaxes with a beer and brushes
that long hair of hers
        and says *You're so beautiful Baby*

A Blood Orange Sky

No trace of breeze, even
the crickets fall silent, hushed
in the static of heat lightning.

Come, my Beloved, let heaven and earth
resolve their differences, while we
feast by candle light on sweet

Cherokee tomatoes, plump
with purple and blush,
gold nectarines

and white peaches, smooth
as alabaster on the tongue,
tart green grapes,

and (most dear of all)
red, juice-dripping blood oranges,
tangy, textured, exotic.

Rue

Sometimes
there are shadows
under the eyes
traces of solitude

no tears
no breath
pain squeezes
lungs into stillness
traps the tongue
behind broken teeth

Pain twists itself
around your throat
bruises your chest
crushes your pelvis
then hangs you
by the entrails:
an example to others

Dandelion Blues

Noise, traffic, potholes,
broken windows, peeling paint,
and alley-stink—

Everyone wants escape:
clean air, blue sky.

The child
who does for himself, he'll get away.
The child whose beauty fades, well . . . .

And that pretty little dandelion
over there surrounded
by cracked asphalt—

that one
singing out she's a sunflower—

Yeah,
be careful to walk around;
you don't want to crush all that heart.

Cargo

He knows
there must be a way
to overcome her fears,

but he's weary
after all this time.
He says

her trust is chipped
at the edges,
bent in the middle.

She's wary
of the gentle hand,
the whispered endearment.

Like a small animal trapped,
she waits for rage and violence
as if that will surely happen,

the only true sign of love.
She steps toward him, he says,
only to step back, afraid

the blow will come,
afraid it won't,
and when they start to argue

he shakes his head,
walks away muttering
about *damaged goods*.

Heat

My lover dreams
of a hot-blooded siren,
humid promises on ruby lips,

        a hungry woman
        with copper hair
        and fire in her eyes

dancing into his famished heart
on sleek stiletto heels,
offering the nectar

        of sweet destruction,
        danger in a red dress
        and glossy vermeil nails

on the hands holding
his ravaged heart.
I've never owned a red dress

        and I won't own one now
        but to say goodbye,
        I shall paint my lips

deep Valentine
and laugh as I walk away,
harboring secrets, turning up the heat.

Love Can Leave Any Time

She rolls over to sleep in his spot
where the habit of his heavier weight
leaves his imprint on the mattress.

The sheets smell like him, still
        damp from a bath, and his pillow
refuses to cradle her head just so,
        resenting any claim of ownership.

The floors snap and creak as the house
settles into the night, the dogs
shift and whimper,

paws racing the air as dream rabbits
        dart away, stay
just out of reach—
        like love will when it feels coy

and decides to prove
it can leave any time it wants,
never mind the damage.

Slow Hand

She should have thought
to thank him for being who he is,
for loving her right to the end,

and she'll remember
when he sang to her,
his smoldering fire, gray eyes,

and that slow hand tracing
the outline of the deep shell
that held her.

She knows when rain falls,
it falls on him too, somewhere.
She wants him to be loved.

She'll remember he likes jazz
on a blue night, that he often
sits alone with the lamp off,

head back, eyes closed, waiting
for the sax to cry, for the drums
to catch the rhythm of his heart.

Mannequin

for Beth, San Diego, Summer 1970

Her own parade, she moves
        down the street, skirts rustling,
scarves or bright ribbons in her hair,
        bangle bracelets jingling, an envy
of high fashion in her Salvation Army treasures.
        She finds lace shawls, a pink boa,
funky hats and leather sandals.
        Every day she is reinvented,
mysterious and beautiful.

She loves dancing and having friends over;
        she never drives a car, doesn't even
have a license, yet always gets where
        she's going and home again by dawn.

She has perfected the grand entrance;
        gaping wounds bandaged with leather
and lace. Feathers and glitter camouflage
        indiscretions; brittle laughter disguises
the gasp of the mortally wounded.

Genesis, Exodus, Leviticus, Numbers

All that summer, he would
greet us at the door as if he'd been
the lost one just now found,

happily setting out dinner plates,
filling them with chicken and biscuits,
and *Please, eat, eat! Want another beer?*
Want to spend the night?

After supper he'd offer conversation,
leaving the living room every few minutes
for a taste, his bottle in a cabinet
behind the peanut butter.

Family tales filled the evening
until he drifted into the books
of the Bible, repeating them in order,
over and over, a mantra:
Genesis, Exodus, Leviticus, Numbers.

My friends would fall silent.
I'd usher them from the house,
back to the car, away from L.A.,
away from my drunk uncle.

This Is For That Arizona Girl

for Maura, San Diego, Summer 1970

the one with the slim copper legs
and long, sun-gold hair, green eyes
sharp as her tongue
and a perfect pink mouth every man
wanted to kiss or bruise.

She showed up one midsummer day
unannounced, a silhouette back-lit
in the center of the old screen door.
She'd hitched rides from Phoenix
to play in seaside Eden, promising to be
not too much trouble. A key
to the door, a word of advice:
for a ride back to the house, call.

Off she went for beer and dancing.
Stars fell from the sky,
Moon kissed the morning sun,
but that Arizona girl never reclaimed
her backpack, her sleeping bag,
the half-finished letter to her mother.

While the small house waited and worried,
a stranger silver-tongued her into his car,
drove down a freeway groping for bare breast,
a touch of tender thigh, then flung open a door
and pushed, and that Arizona girl flew, hit
pavement and bounced, repelling the crush
of oncoming wheels with her young, perfect body,
the only armor she had against an imperfect world.

Moving Violations

Her lover loves
the danger of discovery—
        copping a feel
under the table at the diner,
        a quickie in the washroom
aboard the ferry,
        dirty dancing in the park,
a bit of drama at the theater
        or quiet, shivering sin
in the confessional.

For the annual party at the boss' home
        she wears no bra, no panties;
lunch and shopping in midtown
        and she wears only
a faux fur coat and heels.

Head bobbing, she leans
        into his lap, and they fly
along Coast Highway, red Corvette
        hitting 75 in a 55 zone,
everyone on the Greyhound
        looking down as the bus driver
gives it all he's got, to ride alongside
        the greatest show on earth,
until flashing lights and sirens
        pull them all to the side of the road—
silent, grinning like little ferrets.

Days Of Love

Tell me there will be time for us—
that a few days here or there
wantonly tossed away

will not fly back like raptors
to swallow us
some moonless night.

Tell me that hours spent apart,
moments of anger, minutes
recklessly squandered,

won't leap up to haunt us
when we fall, vulnerable,
into slumber.

Make me believe
there will be time for us,
days and days of sunlight and love.

Thin Girl

I never see her now, that thin girl.
I used to— she would look at me
with those green eyes,

never saying out loud
please think I'm pretty,
please love me.

That thin girl loved music, dancing.
She would say *inside the music*
there is only dance, only air, only light.

I, too, listen to music, though
my old bones don't dance.
As if dust stirs the quiet, I hear

soft taps and clicks as the thin girl's
shoes cross the smooth floor.
She steps, spins, sways,

    that thin girl
    who smiled shyly at the young men
    and danced away into the music,
    leaving only cool, still air.

Hollow Man

He was a handsome mystery
with his dark curls
and those wounded eyes—
        She fell hard.

Too late, he said he had a wife in Toronto.
He said he had two paintings
in an uptown gallery there.
He said he grew up in that beautiful,
fierce city—
        and one day after school
        he'd returned to an empty house:

no farewell note or forwarding address,
no one sent for him, no one returned,
so he stayed until the rent was due.

A hollow boy, this man-child ran
the wild streets with other throw-away kids,
needles in their arms, pools of pain
where their eyes should be.

He said, *show me love,*
but every kindness evaporated
like sweat from torn sheets.

Love couldn't touch him:
it beat against him, fell
at his feet gasping, exhausted.

The Razor Side Of Winter

Hunger bangs hard
against ribs, thirst
taunts her throat.

Fear clings like sweat
and she cannot escape
the stench.

The razor side of winter
drags down, will scrape
her bones smooth,

leaving no sign that she once
knew love and fine linens.

The Dowager's Tale

I can tell you tales, Tanté said,
stories of my young men—
they were such *beautiful* young men.

Ah, my gentle Andres, my
gorgeous Andres. I was living on
the Swan Princess one summer, out
of Stockholm. Andres was the purser;
such a smile, such sleepy eyes!

I'd been ill the whole winter before,
and Papa worried I'd never make it through,
I was so pale and weak— which is why
he insisted on the cruise, you know.

Well, Papa in the room right across
and Andres gloriously naked in my bed,
can you imagine—we were so deliciously
naughty and then, of course,

the gawd-awful giggles start, and once
that happens, it's a lost cause, you just
can't be quiet and we just *knew* Papa
would burst through the door—

and Andres, such a lover,
and he's loving *me*— in three languages
and such moves, a dancer, a gymnast,
and oh, my sweet, sweet Andres, always

knowing exactly what I want, what
I need and well, it was one hot summer
I'll tell you, all that loving and laughter
and dodging Papa

who, of course, thought the cruise
was just the very thing I'd needed
because didn't my eyes look bright
and didn't I seem so happy!

Chasing The Dragon

for Monte

All the love in the world
couldn't make them whole, broken
as they were before they met.

He was lost inside a hole in his arm,
and she got swept downstream.

By now, he's bound to be in prison
or dead—
No one's seen him in a shelter,
there's no sign of him on the street.

She's given up her anger.
Like scalding sand it ran through her fingers,
falling onto the floor in great dunes of sorrow,

so that the grit of it is now worn down, worn in—
a silica painting brushed in the colors of regret.

Rendezvous

Arms and legs entwined,
we lay cocooned for hours in winter,

listening to wind
whistle through old rafters,

knowing the back stairs
had disappeared under all that snow

and only
the very determined could find us.

In spring, we followed train tracks
from our neighborhood to the river.

Half-naked on a blanket
we soaked up sun,

drank *Baby Duck* between tokes,
hidden in the flowers

and new-leafed trees,
and the wild invisibility of our dreams.

Burden Of Love

She remembers when he loved her,
before he ran into David on the bus
after work; yes, his David from Toronto,

who wants to stay high, to replay
back in the day on endless loop,
while Marie and the baby wait, alone

for hours in a basement flat.
David from Toronto—
like brothers, they'd shared

homelessness and hunger through
the same syringe, ridden twin
tie-dyed ponies across the same
psychedelic bridge.

Her man fell from his pony, landed
at the devil's door, did his time
and swore he'd never leave her.

She remembers when he loved her,
but now his voice is brittle and his words
slash, bits of scorn glint in the wound

of his meaning.
How d' I know I give ya' that fat belly?
Somewhere between the hiss and the snarl,

she catches her breath, refuses to cry.
Not so long ago she'd trusted this man,
believed she'd finally come home.

When she leaves
she'll say a prayer for David's Marie.
She'll carry away the burden of love
and a heart at once empty and too full.

Hopeless Romantic

As the bus slowly pulls out
        away from the parking bay,
his last words bounce off window glass
        and fall, orphaned, onto damp concrete.

A half-block from the bus depot, a red light,
        a left turn, across the bridge, ride into the night.
In three days I'll forget the sound of his voice,
        but his eyes will ride the faces

of other young men
        with dark curls, black boots.
In a week, I'll forget most of his lies,
        but I'll see his reflection
in the windows of shops along the street.

In some small town, I'll fall in love
        every Saturday night.
The jukebox'll play, lonesome eyes
        will dare me, dark curls 'n black boots
will string me along.

Second-Hand Apology

Mary and I sit at the table in her kitchen
drinking tea, pushing cookie crumbs away
from the edges of the blue tablecloth.

He told me, she says, how he watched you leave:
Like tiny diamonds, tears glistened
on her cheeks as she turned to get into the cab
and the driver pulled her away from me, swinging
out from the curb, wheels slushing through rain
and last night's snow.

He said he'd bet you promised yourself
you wouldn't cry; much later, of course,
he realized how cruel he'd been, how foolish.

Don't think that none of it mattered.
It all mattered, every bit of it, even
the nights I didn't come home. I began
to miss her before she looked at me
with leaving in her eyes, and I refused
to love her just because she wanted me to.

Mary and I sit at her table drinking tea.
You should forgive him, Mary says.

To Lay Down A Stone

He amused her with stories of a wider world
and pledged to keep her safe.

He promised to cherish, then broke her trust
and the bones of her children.

After all these years, only her shadow moves
through each day—
        her people are gone now,
        back to the dust from whence they came;
        her sickly son, runaway daughter,
        offer no comfort.

Her mister, so coarse, so cruel,
will surely outlive her, though

his will be the saddest farewell—
for when his mortal frame dissolves

into the next life, no one will mourn,
as the breeze wings in a great sigh of relief
        and not one soul
        shall rise to say a kind word,
        to rattle heaven's gate,
        or lay down a stone.

Bourbon & Velvet

His voice was bourbon,
poured straight, no ice.
You had to lean in
to catch each word.

Hard luck dogged his every step
but he fed six kids and a wife.
We were both spoken for,
but I could imagine those

long-fingered hands, rough velvet
to skin, that French tongue in places
a tongue should never be, his voice
rich with promises and prayers.

He'd never leave her
and I'd not give up my life
for half a heart, empty holidays,
and no right to mourn at the end.

What a time we had though—
teasing desire, daring the flames
so keen to tear up the bed,
burn the sheets.

And The Beat Goes On

with apologies to Sonny & Cher

He's been praying love
will step out of the shadows:
his *soul mate.*

All he's got to do is buy the dinner
and drinks, dance real close, tell her
she's pretty, be a gracious escort.
The *right one* will happen along.

She's been praying love
will step out of the shadows:
her *dream come true.*

She can cook, if it gets down to it,
but chooses her restaurants with flair
and her music with a moody finesse.
The *right one* will happen along.

They run for the bus,
        rush to work,
        stand in line, buy a látte,
order lunch,
        retrieve the dry cleaning,
        pick up groceries,
cross the street,
        flag down a cab,
        go to a play,
browse at the book store
        stand in the rain,
        waiting . . . .

Leaving

When I want to leave him
my heart mourns the loss,
aches with the need
for timely decision, hard choice.

Once we were lovers.
Now promises are worn thin
from neglect, trust fell away,
unravelled at the seams.

We are left here,
like birds with broken wings;
we cannot fly together
yet find it impossible to part.

When I want to leave him
my heart feels at once betrayer
and betrayed—

like leaves and their trees,
to disentangle one branch
will grieve another;

to pull at a root
will disarrange nerves
and the seedlings of hope,

and when I want to leave him
I cannot walk forward
nor turn back,

but must stand as if chained
to the wind, imprisoned by Eros
sighing, *A promise is a promise.*

He Loves Her, Loves Her Not

She wakes and watches him
dress, the well defined jawline,
muscular shoulders, narrow waist.

As the sun comes up, he leans
to kiss her, and with a dimpled grin,
is off for his place and a shave,

a clean shirt, before going to work
where the guys will ask,
Get lucky last night?

but he won't tell, just that grin,
trailing mystery to his office,
the water cooler, the copy room,
and his twelve-forty-five
luncheon appointment.

A Portrait, Still Breathing

After all these years
I still feel his hunger
his restlessness
hot breath on my neck

I know well
the tooth of his anger
and can still call up
the ripe, orange heat
of his desire—

the weight of his body
like a promise
hanging motionless
against the stars
in a pale sky

Love Still Warm

Her name
is the sound
of poetry
smooth syllables
carved to curve
around
a man's thoughts

Her scent
is sun
and salt
her touch
at midnight
electrifies
fresh
cool
linens
rustle
skin
whispers
against skin

Sometimes
when
she wakes
she feels
his love
still warm
like breath
on neck
hands
on thigh
tongue tracing
circle of nipple

and
she cannot
let him go
must carry him
with her
all day

A secret

He rides
inside her

yes
inside

teasing
the fire

She Tells Herself

she only wants to know
if he is safe, doing well—

but she really wants to know
if he thinks of her, if he remembers
when the two of them were *us* and *we*.

Does Sorrow wrap blue arms
around him on rainy nights,
as he drinks his whiskey neat,

or does another long-legged girl
slip into the room and curl next to him,
lamplight chasing through her hair?

No Man's Land

That first look—
        and both of you are trapped in *if only*.

Sometimes it's easy because you know
you'll see each other only in this place,
at this luncheon or this conference. You'll speak
only once or three times, then it'll be over—
and you can stand it for that long.

It can be more difficult, of course,
but you get through it
without bending, without breaking.
Later, you think how lucky it was

the crisis averted, will power
and integrity held the fort.
Much later—

years later, you write a poem
not because you regret
but because you remember.

Southern Comfort

She walks home from the diner
on aching feet, pockets jingling with tips.

Through open windows she hears him play guitar
or recite poetry, with the notes

from a plaintive sax tumbling out
of cheap speakers and riding the breeze

for another half block.
Once, while looking at his yellowed ceiling,

he cried out *Stel-la!* as if his heart were
near breaking, and she held him tight

in her sleep that night. When
he cannot rest, the sounds of lives

running full-out fill his rooms.
A woman's laughter ricochets against

his window sill as he tilts back a cold,
long-necked beer, a sheen of sweat

on his chest.
Down here, look at me, she wants to shout,

her heart turned shy, her tongue
suddenly frozen in the summer heat.

At The Airport

Tucson, Arizona

They came early to catch their flight,
        that young woman and her man.
Two children trailed after—
        The girl looked like her mother,
who was pretty before fear pinched her face,
        stole the sparkle from her eyes.

The boy, maybe nine, too thin,
        whispered a plea to his mother:
a drink, please, water will do.
        The mother folded into herself
until she was as small as she could be,
        then asked her man,
a drink for the boy, please, water will do.
        The man's broad-shouldered voice
snarled, *Not Now! Not Now!*

With tension riding a lined brow,
        anger tightening his shoulders,
he led his flock to the boarding gate.
        They followed him, the three of them,
wary, obedient.

Faux

He bought her a faux leather purse
and a pair of shoes to match.
They went well with her new dress
and sweater set.

He bought her a gold-tone necklace
with a rhinestone centerpiece.
It sparkled under bright light
if she turned just so.

He bought her a split-level,
the one on the corner with
the tiny yard, hard against
a brick wall blocking

traffic just beyond.
She'd wanted flowers
but he said the price was right.

He gave her three children
in quick succession, got home late
every Monday, Wednesday and Friday,
and when she dared ask for warmth,

he told her to turn up the thermostat
a notch and count her blessings,
after all, hadn't he given her
everything?

If He Cried

That one,
with the ribbon in her hair,
she's married to him—
        yes, over there.

Look at those dark eyes of his,
        like pools of lava
and you know if he cried
        (he never would, but if he did)
the tears would break your heart,
        pouring out like tiny diamonds
from the bottom of his soul,

and you wouldn't be able to hold your ground
no matter what the argument.
        You'd fall, legs splayed out from under you
        and nothing to grab onto,
those tears ripping your whole center apart
so you know, she must be very careful
not to hurt him.

He Tends Roses Now

forgiving thorns
for the sake of fragrant
blossoms,

allowing for variety,
even contradiction,
in a garden

where once only
sunburnt weeds grew,
squeezed between stones.

He tends roses
with quiet conversation
and tactful persuasion,

sharing his heart
in ways he never thought
to share with her.

We Meet At The Sand's Edge Café

and he wants me to sit with him,
drink cool tea and talk. The sea
will rush forward and back

just beyond our small table,
as we speak of where we've been
and what we've done all these years,

and how good we both look—
he in a new shirt, me in a new dress—
as if we intended to impress.

He wants me to sit with him,
drink cool tea and desire him again.
He wants us to make love all afternoon,

go for a late dinner, make love
until dawn, then sleep, entwined:
children who know their place in the world.

The Devil Pounds The Door

        and he'll have you.
I haven't the power to bargain
or grant dispensation for your sins.

To have a drunken father
bestows no right to *be* a drunken father,
to have a neglectful mother—

well, excuses rain down
until we are deafened
by the clamor.

I'm sorry it's come to this, Cousin,
but the devil pounds the door
with neither mercy

nor forgiveness in his pocket
and he comes for the man you are,
not the man you could have been.

Pantry Passion

The spoon was sexy but cunning,
waiting to scoop out any remaining
crumbs of trust.

The mixer, flashy and a good dancer,
offered plenty of spinning and whirring,
but was *so* shallow.

The Dutch oven was packed with surprises,
often hot tempered, and the shy ladle was serious,
with an artistic flair, and fiercely possessive.

The coffee mug was full of himself; still lived
in the nook with the slender, perking pot,
and spied on the tea cup when she was alone.

I married the can opener. He has scared me
a time or two, bending rules, chewing
on something new—
        but such energy,
        the hum and bite of his passion!

Shield & Spear

Love is not timid but fierce, even righteous,
hooking her nails into flesh and sinew,
biting into bone, not about to let go.

Love is not silent, nor gentle or blind.
Love comes hurtling out of the East
on a lathered pony, hard-ridden

and wicked as a summer storm.
Love demands and mountains move,
trembling before her advance.

No child, once loved,
ever travels alone:
Love's memory is at once
shield and spear.

Pulse

The horns
are overcome as
the sax starts to weep
and the drums
leave echos of bass notes
an angry pulse-thrum
around the room

The strings reach out
to soothe but begin to sob
in sympathy with the sax
and the drumbeat
escalates
grinding bits of anger
into the floor
leaving tune scraps
and song phrases
on the polished surface

The evening cracks
wide open as the horns
clarinet and trumpet
step up
then step back
as the sax moans
wails
can't hold it all in
and notes fly
through the open window
and the melody turns bashful
with love but kind of melancholy
like after too much wine

Always, That River

is right out there, so close
it can threaten or soothe depending
on its mood and the color of the sky.

Sliding by just past the door,
that river sings hyms, hurls curses,
rides smooth as glass, floats logs.
Storm-riled, it traps souls, drags
off what it can find—

and what it finds, it keeps for its own.
It'll keep for its own the one who needed faith
but didn't know its name;

that river'll forever hold the one who wanted
forgiveness but didn't know how to pray
or when to kneel before the altar of sacrifice.

It'll never give up the one who craved love
but didn't understand it had to be given away.
At once mother and lover,

the river's current is a dark companion
who never sleeps, but counts its trophies
each night and counts them dear—
right there, just past the door.

About The Author

Lorraine Merrin, a child of the desert, now lives in the Pacific Northwest with her husband and two large dogs. She is quite happy with green trees and rain, though wishes the dogs would wipe their paws and dry off before entering the house after a good winter run.